A Basic Training, Caring & Understanding Library

Your Healthy Puppy

Approved by the A.S.P.C.A.

Patricia S. Lehman

Published in association with T.F.H. Publications, Inc.,
the world's largest and most respected publisher of pet literature

Chelsea House Publishers
Philadelphia

A Basic Training, Caring & Understanding Library

Kitten and Cat Care
Healthy Skin & Coat: Cats
The Myth & Magic of Cats
Persian Cats
Feline Behavior
Obedience Training
The Well-Trained Dog
Adopting a Dog
The Perfect Retriever
Healthy Skin & Coat: Dogs
Traveling With Dogs
Training Older Dogs
Housebreaking & Other Puppy Problems
Puppy Care and Training
Your Healthy Puppy
Perfect Children's Dogs
Training Your Puppy
You & Your Puppy

Publisher's Note: All of the photographs in this book have been coated with FOTOGLAZE™ finish, a special lamination that imparts a new dimension of colorful gloss to the photographs.

Reinforced Library Binding & Super-Highest Quality Boards

135798642
Library of Congress Cataloging-in-Publication Data applied for 0-7910-4818-7.

YOUR HEALTHY PUPPY

by Patricia S. Lehman

yearBOOKS,INC.

Dr. Herbert R. Axelrod,
Founder & Chairman

Dominique De Vito
Chief Editor

Carolynne Van Houten
Editor

yearBOOKS are all photo composed, color separated and designed on Scitex equipment in Neptune, N.J. with the following staff:

DIGITAL PRE-PRESS

Patricia Northrup
Supervisor

Robert Onyrscuk
Jose Reyes

COMPUTER ART

Patti Escabi
Sandra Taylor Gale
Candida Moreira
Joanne Muzyka
Francine Shulman

ADVERTISING SALES

Nancy S. Rivadeneira
Advertising Sales Director
Cheryl J. Blyth
Advertising Account Manager
Amy Manning
Advertising Director
Sandy Cutillo
Advertising Coordinator

©yearBOOKS, Inc.
1 TFH Plaza
Neptune, N.J. 07753
Completely manufactured in
Neptune, N.J.
USA

Cover design by Sherise Buhagiar

Approximately 250,000 puppies are born each year who will need good homes and lots of love and attention. As a pet owner, you will certainly want to ensure that the puppy you select grows up happy and healthy, and in the most secure environment you are able to provide. This yearBOOK is designed as a handy reference, offering accurate and up-to-date advice and information to help you make informed decisions about raising your new puppy, and establishing a trusting and lasting relationship.

What Are yearBOOKS?

Because dog ownership continues to grow at a rapid pace, information regarding canine health is vitally needed in the marketplace. Books, the usual way information is transmitted, can be too slow. Sometimes, by the time a book is written and published, the material is a year or two old, and no new text has been added during that time.

A book in magazine form can best accommodate breaking stories and the most current information. We have adopted certain magazine publishing techniques in the creation of this yearBOOK to make the format streamlined and easy to read. It is also much less expensive than books due to advertising support. To combine these assets into a great publication, we've issued this yearBOOK in both magazine and book formats, and made it available at different prices.

How could anyone resist an adorable gift basket like this?

CONTENTS

Contributing Photographers: Linda Willard, Shirley Farrington, Lindy Sander, Mary-Elizabeth Simpson, Patricia F. Lehman.

One thing is for certain: The love you give your new puppy will be returned unconditionally.

Puppies are irresistible. Their winsome expressions and wagging tails tug at our heartstrings. Within their innocence, we see promise. Puppies represent the future; our hopes, desires, goals, and dreams. The awkward youngster may grow into the handsome show dog. The free spirit may develop into the obedience champion. The adopted pet may become the best friend. Puppies reflect our vision of the world around us. In their eyes we see love; in their hearts, trust; in their actions, respect.

Because you're reading this book, one can assume you've recently acquired a puppy or are considering adding one to

You may want to photograph each stage of your puppy's growth, because, as is true for many breeds, he won't stay little for long!

your family. Congratulations on being a responsible owner!

A dog can live 15 or more years, so it's important to think about the obligations as well as the benefits involved in ownership. Remember, the energetic youngster you fell in love with will soon become the unruly adolescent. The dignified adult will mature into the silver-muzzled senior. There-

Attending dog shows can expose you to a variety of dogs, and help you select the breed of your choice.

fore, all members of the family must be committed to exercising, training, feeding, and grooming the dog, and providing him with proper veterinary care throughout his lifetime. If you're thinking of purchasing a four-legged companion for your children, keep in mind that most tasks will fall to the adults. Are you willing to take over the child's duties when he or she forgets or is busy?

Puppies require constant attention and supervision, even when you have other priorities for your time. However, the diligence you put into building this special

This English Bulldog puppy boasts a camouflaged display in its distinctive markings.

relationship will be more than repaid by the loyalty and devotion your dog gives you in return.

THE RIGHT DOG FOR YOU

The process of selecting a healthy puppy begins long before you visit a kennel or view a litter. It starts even before the puppy's birth, as you undertake the meticulous process of learning about dogs and their traits, locating a reputable breeder, and picking the right pet for you. Perhaps you already know the breed you desire, or have narrowed your choice to size, coat type, and appearance. Possibly you're looking for a dog like the one you remem-

child can control? Dogs also vary in color, coat, and grooming requirements. Some shed profusely, others very little. Do you mind a dusting of hair on furniture, clothing and carpets? Does someone in the family suffer from allergies? Do you have the time and money to groom a dog with a complicated hairstyle?

Perhaps the greatest differences among breeds are their instinctive personality traits. Most dogs were bred to perform specific functions: retrieving birds, herding livestock, killing vermin, pulling sleds, or guarding property. The American Kennel Club, for example, recognizes dogs in the Sporting, Working, Hound, Terrier, Toy, Non-Sporting, and Herding groups. Yet, although few modern animals work for their livings, they often continue to exhibit the inherent characteristics of their breed. Don't be surprised if your Lab puppy carries stray socks throughout the house, your little Westie ferociously attacks his squeaky toy, or your Corgi nips at your heels. To find out more about the more historical backgrounds of dogs, consult one of the more comprehensive guides, such as *The Atlas of Dog Breeds of the World* (T.F.H. Publications, Inc.)

The benefits of companionship and camaraderie have convinced more and more pet owners to take home more than one puppy.

ber from childhood, or one that appealed to you at a show.

Currently, more than 400 breeds are known worldwide. From the tiny Chihuahua to the majestic Great Dane, the feisty terrier to the easygoing retriever, a dog exists to fulfill the expectations of almost any owner. To find the breed that is best suited to your lifestyle,

personality, and environment, it's important to weigh a variety of factors. Dogs differ in size, strength, energy level, and need for exercise. Are you looking for a canine athlete to join you on your daily runs, or a quiet pet to keep you company at home? Can you handle a powerful breed, or do you prefer a pet that even a small

6

The Labrador Retriever is known for its gentle temperament and consistent loyalty.

ADOPTING A MIXED-BREED PUPPY

For a devoted family companion, you might consider a mixed-breed puppy. By taking your time and making a careful selection, you can find a mixed breed that is just as friendly, intelligent, and healthy as a purebred. In fact, some experts believe these dogs are actually healthier, and enjoy greater longevity, due to their mixed parentage. This is because there is less likelihood in an outcross mating of recessive genes combining to cause disease.

The main drawback in choosing a mixed-breed is the uncertainty involved in bringing together different traits. It's hard to predict adult characteristics in mixed-breed puppies. In addition, you may not know how the puppy was raised or what type of handling he received.

If you decide to adopt an animal from a shelter, look for a lively, alert puppy who is interested in people. Ask to observe and play with him in a holding area away from his cage, or take him for a walk around the building. How does the puppy respond to you? Is he the type of pet you would want in your home? Visit the shelter more than once before making your decision, and don't hesitate to keep looking for that perfect canine best friend.

WHERE TO BUY YOUR PUPPY

To acquire a purebred puppy, it's vital to deal only with reputable breeders who

Create a healthy environment before acquiring your puppy, and he will adjust to his new home much more quickly.

raise their animals with love, gentleness, and plenty of human interaction. You can start your search by contacting the AKC for the current address of the national breed parent club. Most organizations offer information packets for prospective owners and can supply addresses of local clubs and breeders. You may also find breeders through veterinarians, groomers, training instructors, or boarding kennels. Many local clubs know reliable breeders, and some provide a referral service by telephone.

Another method of finding a quality puppy is to attend a dog show—an all-breed event, or, better yet, a specialty show that features the breed you're considering. Visiting a show is especially helpful if you have questions or are thinking about a rare breed that may be difficult to track down locally. It's important to view adult dogs, as well as puppies, before making your

Breeders often advise potential owners to meet a puppy's parents in order to perceive the litter's potential.

Your veterinarian, local groomer or trainer are all reliable sources in recommending a reputable breeder.

choice. Dogs often look different from their photographs. Meeting a dog close-up gives you a better idea of whether it fits your family's needs. Always purchase the show catalog, so you can contact breeders whose dogs interest you.

Handlers, too, may know whether breeders have puppies available. While you're at the show, don't overlook the obedience ring. Observing the dogs competing in these specialized tests, and learning which kennels produced them, can help you locate an intelligent, trainable pet.

Once you have narrowed your list of possible kennels, you can contact breeders with specific information about the kind of puppy you

desire. Do you mainly want a family pet? Are you planning to show or breed your dog? Do you prefer a certain color, marking pattern, or coat type? Make appointments to visit several kennels before you decide where to purchase your puppy. Don't buy the first one you come across. In fact, some buyers prefer to talk to breeders without seeing the puppies at all.

First, meet the adult dogs, including the puppies' mother, and inspect the premises. Are they clean and well-maintained? Are the dogs in good condition? Are they friendly, interested, and eager to greet visitors? Never buy from a kennel where the adults are aggressive or overly timid. The temperaments of the grown dogs offer a strong

indication of the puppies' future personalities.

Be sure to discuss any problems that occur in the breed and find out whether the breeder has had the parent animals tested for known hereditary disorders. Common tests, depending on the breed involved, include eye examinations for progressive retinal atrophy (PRA), radiographs for hip and elbow displasia, and blood tests for von Willebrand's disease. Responsible breeders should have certificates available to show buyers from the Canine Eye Registry Foundation (CERF), the Orthopedic Foundation for Animals (OFA), PennHip, or other disease-specific organizations.

Ask to see the puppies' pedigree and look for show, obedience, or performance titles. This will give some indication of how closely they meet the breed standard and whether you can count on good temperament. The breeder should also be able to provide information on previous litters, including titles the dogs have earned, health status, personality traits, and life spans. Go over the terms of the sales contract, and find out whether the breeder provides a written health guarantee. Will he or she offer a refund or replacement puppy if a problem is found? Will veterinary expenses be reimbursed? What provisions will be made if you're already attached to the pet? Some breeders require that pet-quality puppies be neutered before they submit registration papers. This makes any resulting litters ineligible for registration.

"Eenie, meenie, miney, moe"—Each of these Irish Setter pups would make a wonderful addition to a loving household.

In a rare display, this Collie pup sits still long enough to strike a stunning pose in a formal portrait.

Make certain you understand all of the terms of the contract before you take the puppy home. Finally, be patient in your search. Responsible breeders may not breed every year and most have waiting lists for their most promising animals. Waiting for a quality puppy is never a mistake.

WHAT TO LOOK FOR IN A BREEDER

- Knowledgeable about the breed, its good and bad points
- Member of a breed or kennel club
- Adheres to the club's code of ethics
- Carefully plans each mating to improve the breed
- Tests breeding stock for heredity diseases
- Breeds only physically and mentally sound animals
- Raises puppies in a home environment
- Facilities clean; adult dogs and puppies clean and well-groomed
- Allows buyer to see adult dogs
- Puppies never released before eight weeks or the appropriate age for the breed
- Provides pedigree and registration papers
- Offers written contract and health guarantee
- Willing to answer buyer's questions
- Helps buyer select the right puppy for his or her needs
- Takes back a dog if the owner is unable to keep it
- Gives references
- Requires neutering of pet-quality dogs
- Remains interested in the puppy's welfare after the sale

Crates offer puppies a private "den" of their own.

SELECTING A HEALTHY PUPPY

Puppies who are healthy—physically and mentally—are happy, lively, playful, and friendly. Their energy, enthusiasm, and *joie de vivre* allow them to adapt to new environments with assurance and confidence. To find your perfect puppy, make an appointment to see the litter when the puppies are likely to be awake and active. You'll want to observe their interaction with each other, as well as with you alone. Often, one will stand out as the friendliest, cutest, or most affectionate. He may come right to you to greet you. Many owners make a successful match with the "love-at-first-sight" method of choosing a puppy. However, don't overlook quieter youngsters. They often "bloom" away from their littermates, when they relax and settle down in their new homes.

Once you have found a puppy you like, inspect him carefully from head to tail for any signs of illness. Are the eyes clear and bright, with no discharge or cloudiness? The nose cool and moist? The ears clean and odor-free? If the puppy scratches or shakes his head, he might have ear mites or a possible infection. Do the teeth meet in the correct bite for the breed? Have the baby teeth come in properly? Is the puppy's coat thick, shiny, and clean? A dry, flaky coat, or one with bald patches, suggests the presence of mites, fleas, allergies, ringworm, or even a poor diet.

Avoid any puppy who coughs, sneezes, vomits, or has diarrhea. Although these problems may be temporary, it could also signal a more serious condition. Find out when the veterinarian last examined the puppy and ask for a health certificate and record of vaccinations and wormings. The breeder should supply a small portion of food, along with complete instructions on how to care for the puppy at home. Many breeders also give owners their puppy's blankets and favorite toys. Make certain you receive the registration form, pedigree, and copies of any contracts or guarantees.

Raising a healthy puppy is demanding and challenging. Your puppy will undoubtedly make mistakes as he adapts to his new home. He will test his limits, as well as your patience. At times, you may feel frustrated and overwhelmed. Remember, your puppy will be little for only a short time. Enjoy it! The attention you provide—and especially the love you give—will make your puppy a pleasure to own.

It's important to check the eyes, ears, and, of course—the nose—before selecting a puppy.

A HEALTHY ENVIRONMENT FOR YOUR PUPPY

It's natural for a puppy to explore his territory. His eyes and ears, and especially his nose, take him into every interesting crevice. Did you forget to put away that new pair of shoes? Any goodies lurking in the chair cushions? Are last night's chicken bones still in the garbage can? All are fair game for the ever-curious youngster! Until now, your little dog has stayed close to his mother and whelping box. She provided the rules for acceptable canine behavior.

This new realm is exciting, challenging, and perhaps a bit scary. It will take time and repetition for your puppy to learn proper manners. At first, he won't be able to distinguish between a doggie toy and a child's favorite doll. He doesn't understand the difference between his newspapers and your best carpet. The first step in raising a puppy, therefore, is to provide a safe place where he can master living in the human world.

PUPPY-PROOFING YOUR HOME

Puppy-proofing begins even before you bring your new puppy home. You'll need to decide where he will eat, play, and sleep. Because puppies usually prefer to be close to family members—their new pack—many owners choose the kitchen for their pet's living quarters. The washable floor is convenient and doorways can be blocked with doggie gates. To inspect the room for hidden hazards, get down to your puppy's eye (or nose) level.

If you offer lots of love and attention, it won't take long for your dog to feel comfortable in his new environment.

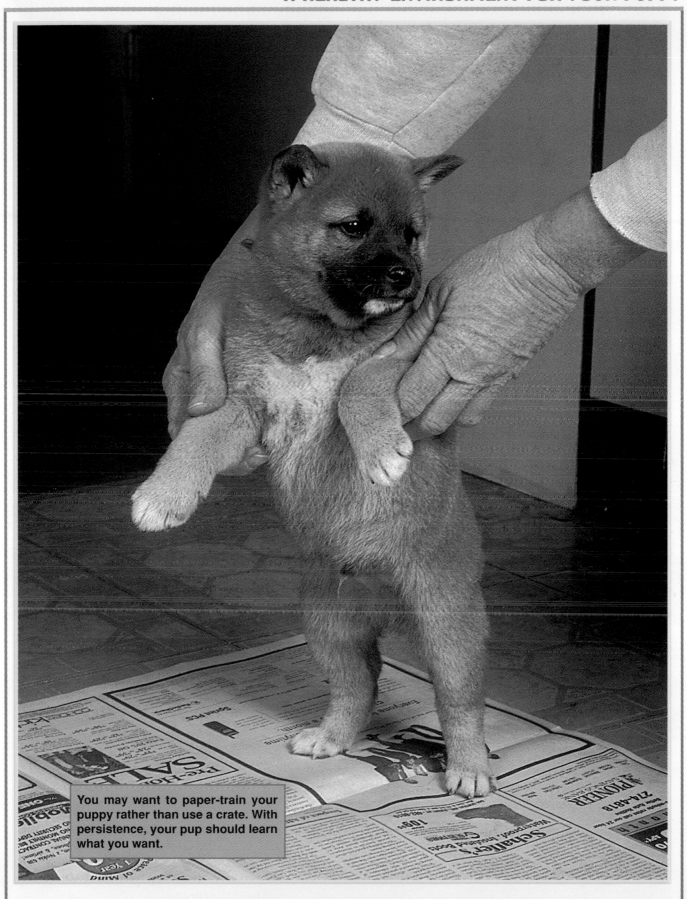

You may want to paper-train your puppy rather than use a crate. With persistence, your pup should learn what you want.

You'll probably find dangers you never noticed before.

Common household items that can harm pets include electric cords, garbage in uncovered cans, toxic cleaning products, and insecticides. Because puppies investigate everything that attracts their attention, you must be vigilant in keeping items out of reach. Don't leave shoes, socks, clothes, or breakables within range of your puppy. Be careful with medicines, cigarettes, and alcoholic beverages. Keep the toilet bowl covered, especially if you use chemical cleaners. Certain house plants, too, may cause serious illness if chewed or swallowed. Watch for stairs, open windows, and balco-

nies. Many pets are injured or killed each year from such falls.

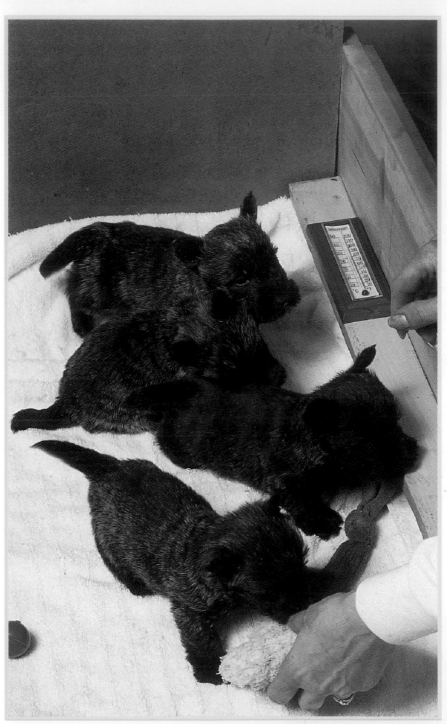

A qualified breeder will provide a safe and secure environment for newborn puppies like these Scotties.

Preparing your home for a puppy is much like getting ready for a baby's arrival.

With planning and common sense, you can protect little ones from dangers they are too young to perceive themselves.

SAFE TOYS

Playing and chewing are a central part of puppyhood, and pet toys come in an amazing variety of sizes, shapes, materials, and types. However, because baby teeth are sharper and more piercing than permanent teeth, it's vital to choose only safe toys. The most durable kinds, such as Nylabone® or Gumabone®, are made of a material that can't break or splinter. Be careful of soft, rubber squeaky toys. These are easily shredded and your puppy may swallow pieces of the toy or squeaker. Surprisingly, tennis balls can be dangerous for animals with strong jaws. The balls can stick in the throat, cutting off the air supply. Some dogs

More than one owner has learned from experience that puppies cannot distinguish between legitimate chew toys and the impostors!

even manage to swallow small balls.

Of course, these toys are safe to use when you're there to supervise your puppy's playtime. Allow plenty of time to play directly with your pet. Toss a ball and teach him to bring it back. Play hide-and-seek with his toy. Let your puppy use his nose to sniff out the hiding place. It's best, however, to limit the number of toys you provide at one time. With an assortment to choose from, it's more difficult for a young dog to understand the difference between his possessions and yours. Play is essential to puppies. It stimulates learning, develops confidence, and is an invaluable first step in all forms of obedience training.

CRATE TRAINING

Part of the instinctive nature of dogs is their desire for small spaces of their own. Like the hidden dens of their ancestors, crates provide a sense of security for dogs. They offer a place where puppies can be safely

There is nothing puppies enjoy more than a vigorous game of tug of war!

It is important to allow your new puppy to become accustomed to a collar for his own protection, and as a tool in training.

left and a private nest where they can let down their guard and relax undisturbed by children or guests. In today's household, crates are an ideal solution for owners who must leave their puppies when they go out. When used properly, crates prevent destruction, and aid in the task of housebreaking. For more detailed information about housebreaking using a crate, see Michael Kelly's *Housebreaking and Training Your New Puppy* (T.F.H. Publications, Inc.).

To successfully train your puppy to use the crate, make the activity pleasant and fun. First, have the crate set up and in place when you bring the youngster home. You may choose a wire crate, which is easy to fold down for dog shows or travel, or a plastic airline-style crate. In fact, if the breeder ships the animal, the crate will arrive with your puppy. Make certain the wires on either style crate are not far enough apart to allow your pet to push his muzzle or legs through the bars. Also, be sure the crate is the correct size.

Many owners choose large enclosures so their dogs will have plenty of room. However, this defeats the crate's purpose for housebreaking because the puppy has enough room to relieve himself and still keep his bed clean. To be useful in housebreaking, the crate should only be large enough for the animal to stand, turn around, and lie down. If your puppy will grow and you don't want to purchase more than one crate, place a partition (available in pet supply stores) inside the crate to give it the appropriate amount of room.

Always proceed slowly, calmly, and gently in training, so you don't frighten your dog. The best way to lure him into his crate is to place a treat or toy inside. Whenever your puppy en-

Puppies are pack animals by nature, a trait assumed from an ancestry with wolves.

These pampered Bichons enjoy the "ritziest" of accommodations.

ters, pet and praise enthusiastically. Then, close the door for a moment or two while he's inside. If your puppy is quiet in the crate, give plenty of praise and open the door. If he protests with crying or whining, tell him "No!" and ignore him until he calms down.

Gradually increase the length of time he stays in the crate. Leave the door open when your puppy is loose and soon you'll find he enters on his own when he wants a nap or quiet time.

Remember, the crate always should be a positive experience. Never use it for punishment. Don't keep your puppy confined for long periods. Young dogs must go outside frequently, so two or three hours is the limit for staying in the crate. If you work full time and can't

come home at midday, consider hiring a neighbor or pet sitter to take out the puppy. Many owners move the crate to the bedroom at night so the puppy can sense his owner's presence while sleeping. This is especially important when your puppy first comes home and misses his mother and littermates. Keeping the crate nearby further helps in housebreaking because you can be alert to his cries and actions.

Crate training will be helpful when your puppy visits the groomer or veterinarian. A crate also makes vacationing more enjoyable. You'll be more likely to find that your dog is welcomed by hotel staff when they know he'll be securely confined. Some lodgings that don't normally accept pets

will allow a well-behaved, crated dog to stay with his owner. If you plan to travel or ship your pet by air, it's vital to allow him time to become accustomed to his crate.

A crate also enhances your pet's safety when he rides in the car. Crates for small breeds can be placed on the car seat and belted in place. Large crates can go in the back of a van or station wagon. In case of an accident, your dog will not be thrown from the vehicle to be injured or killed, nor will he escape and run onto the highway and lost. Some dogs also may display their protective instincts because of fear and anxiety and interfere with the work of rescue personnel. Crates provide an added measure of safety to all involved.

Besides housetraining, crates are useful for trips to the veterinarian, or when traveling on vacation.

THE BIG BACKYARD

One of the considerations in choosing a dog is how much space is available outdoors for play and exercise. Many breeders require that owners have a fenced-in yard or an enclosed kennel run before they sell a puppy. Some will allow pets to go to apartment dwellers if the owners make a commitment to regular walks. Because unexpected dangers exist outdoors, you'll need to puppy-proof the yard as carefully as you did the home.

First, check the fence for any escape routes. Puppies can squeeze through tiny holes and terriers can dig their way out of many enclosures. Make certain the fence goes all the way to the ground and doesn't give when you push on it. It must also be high enough for dogs who'll grow to be large-sized dogs.

Next, examine your property for anything that could sicken or hurt your puppy, such as lawn chemicals, insecticides, bait, traps, weed killers, car products, swimming pools, elevated decks, and wild animals that might enter the yard. Many common outdoor shrubs and trees can cause mouth and throat irritation, vomiting, and even death if a puppy chews or swallows parts of the plant. These include the azalea, holly, yew, oleander, privet hedge, and hydrangea. Even certain flowers and bulbs may cause reactions if eaten.

Finally, provide plenty of fresh water and shelter from the elements. The best way to keep your puppy safe outdoors is to never leave him alone. Not only can stray animals come into the yard, possibly to fight, but also the theft of dogs is a serious problem in many areas.

How does your garden grow? This youngster certainly adds to the scenery.

IDENTIFICATION FOR PUPPIES

To help ensure that your little "escape artist" will be returned if he manages to flee the house or yard, you'll need to use some form of identification. Three popular methods are ID tags, tattoos, and microchips. The conventional

Using the latter helps to protect your privacy and prevent nuisance calls. If you choose a tattoo or microchip for identification, a tag is still important to alert the finder and provide the registry organization where the pet's number is on file.

behind the reputation of the kennel. If you're interested in this form of identification, contact your veterinarian about the best age to tattoo. Many kennel clubs also hold special tattoo clinics.

Tattooing doesn't hurt—it takes about 10 to 15 min-

Identify your beloved companion, and he'll always find his way back home.

ID collar tag is the first step in identifying a lost pet. Most people who find a stray look for a tag before checking for other forms of identification. ID tags come in metal or plastic and some fasten directly on the collar strap. A tag can include your name and phone number, or the 800 telephone number of a national registry service.

However, because collars can break and tags may be lost or stolen, many owners want a permanent form of identification for their pets. The most popular method today is the tattoo. In fact, a puppy already may have a tattoo when he comes from the breeder. This is a sign that he or she cares about the dogs and intends to stand

utes—and anesthesia usually is not necessary. Most dogs are tattooed on the inner thigh or abdomen. The most significant step, however, is to register the code number with one of the national registry organizations. When someone finds a lost pet, he or she calls the 800 number and the registry notifies the owner of the finder's location. Most animal shelter workers are trained to look for tattoos and research laboratories won't experiment on dogs with tattoos. A tattoo also provides proof of ownership if a dog is stolen.

The newest form of permanent identification is the microchip. About the size of a grain of rice, the chip is implanted under the dog's skin between the shoulder blades. The veterinarian inserts it with a syringe, similar to giving an injection. Most animals feel no discomfort. However, sometimes there is bleeding at the site of the injection. Puppies can receive the chip as early as 7 to 10 weeks—as soon as their muscles develop in the area—and may already have one when they come from the breeder. Several companies sell chips and owners can include information about their dogs' health and food requirements in the national databases. The American Kennel Club also has started a program, called *AKC Companion Animal Recovery*, that offers a round-the-clock service for dogs with tattoos or microchips. If someone finds a pet with the AKC collar tag, he or she can call Companion Animal Recovery and give the ID number. The AKC then notifies the owner of the finder's location. Scanners are needed to read chips and obtain identification numbers. The chip maker associated with the AKC's program has given its HomeAgain scanner to all humane organizations. Other manufacturers also provide free scanners to shelters.

Because your puppy can't ask for help or give his address if it gets lost, an ID tag, tattoo, microchip, or combination of methods is critical in helping him find his way back to his family.

Investing in a pet gate can help inquisitive puppies avoid unknown perils—like stairs.

The outside world can appear to be a jungle from your puppy's perspective.

YOUR HEALTHY PUPPY'S DIET

The first year of a puppy's life is characterized by rapid growth and high energy needs. Muscles and bones are developing, cells are forming, and vital processes are taking place within the and amount of food you feed lays the groundwork for future health and a long life-span. It's important there-fore, to choose a high-quality diet made just for growing puppies. Because

BASIC NUTRIENTS

Puppies and adults need five kinds of nutrients, and water. However, depending on age, activity level, environment, and health status, the proper amount and balance will change.

Offering your puppy his meal at the same time and in the same place every day helps to regulate his delicate digestive system. This Sussex Spaniel enjoys a hearty meal.

body. Depending on the breed, a puppy may gain 10 pounds, or 100 pounds, during the first 12 to 18 months. Proper feeding plays a critical role in this body-building process. The type your puppy's digestive system is immature, the food should be easy to digest and dense in energy. It must also contain the correct level of nutrients for this complex stage of growth.

One of the most critical nutrients for young dogs is protein. Found in such animal sources as beef, chicken, fish, and eggs, as well as plant products like grains and soybeans, protein is essential for normal growth, muscle and bone formation, tissue repair, and internal body functions. Protein forms the basic structure of skin, hair, and toenails. It also makes up tendons, ligaments, and muscles.

During digestion, protein is broken down into smaller substances called amino acids. Some of these are made within the body. Others must be supplied by the diet. Most commercial foods use a variety of protein sources to ensure that they provide all the required amino acids. The higher the protein's quality, the smaller the amount needed overall.

Your puppy's diet should contain at least 29 percent protein. If it does not supply enough, skeletal disorders such as hip dysplasia may develop. Other conditions resulting from too little protein include poor growth, weight loss, skin and hair problems, and lower resistance to disease.

Carbohydrates from grain and vegetable sources provide animals with energy. The sugar in carbohydrates is carried to the liver, where it's changed into glycogen and stored for future energy demands. Carbohydrates also supply fiber, which plays a key role in the digestive process. Some types of fiber are useful when dogs have diarrhea or constipation. Others help to lower the level of cholesterol in the blood. Because it can decrease the absorption of nutrients, foods designed for growth are fairly low in fiber. However, digestible carbohydrates remain essential to the growing puppy. If his diet contains too little of this vital food group, the body will substitute protein for energy needs, leading to the potential for protein deficiency.

Another important source of energy is dietary fat. Fat provides more than twice the energy, per unit, as protein and carbohydrates. Fat also aids the absorption of vitamins A, D, E, and K, and supplies the essential fatty acid, linoleic acid. Puppies can develop a fatty acid deficiency from eating a poor-quality or low-fat diet. Signs of FAD include slow development, weight loss, flaky skin, and a dull coat. Most foods for growth contain 21 to 24

These two are about to enjoy a balanced meal designed just for their growing needs.

These Newfoundland puppies show that drinking can be a cooperative effort.

percent fat. Too much fat is harmful as well, leading to weight gain and nutritional imbalances.

Puppies also need vitamins and minerals to develop correctly. Vitamins are organic compounds that serve as coenzymes to help control internal body processes. Minerals form the structural components of bones and teeth. They also help to regulate blood chemistry and maintain the balance of water within the cells. The best way to make certain that your pet receives these nutrients is to choose a high-quality food, guaranteed on the label to be complete and balanced.

Further supplementation is not necessary and may even be harmful.

Researchers have found that excesses and imbalances of calcium and phosphorus can cause skeletal problems in growing dogs. Puppies may develop lameness, broken bones, and abnormal bone formation. Too much calcium, combined with overeating, also contributes to the potentially life-threatening stomach disorder known as *bloat* in large, deep-chested breeds. Be sure to check with your veterinarian before adding vitamins or minerals to the diet. If you believe the food

is inadequate, switch to a better product.

Surprisingly, the most vital nutrient for puppies—and adults—is water. Dogs can survive several days without food. However, a loss of only 10 to 15 percent of body water can lead to serious illness and even death. The thirst response will increase or decrease, depending on the type of food your pet eats, salt intake, exercise, weather, and basic temperament. Make certain you provide clean, fresh water every day. If you notice your puppy is drinking more or less than usual, consult the veterinarian. This may be a sign of illness.

A breeder or veterinarian can recommend a dog food that is specially formulated for the growing puppy.

KINDS OF FOOD

When you pick up your new puppy from the breeder, you should receive a portion of the food he's been eating, along with instructions on when and how much to feed. Depending on his or her experience with dogs and their response to different diets, this may be a dry, canned, or soft-moist product. Each has advantages and disadvantages, depending on your pet's needs and your personal preferences.

Dry food, introduced in the late 19th century as an offshoot of the cereal industry, is the most popular method of feeding. Many commercial kennels use dry food and a number of premium brands are available. Its advantages include convenience, ease of preparation and storage, and cost. Because of its low water content, you pay only for the food ingredients rather than fancy packaging.

Most of the nutrients in dry food come from cereal grains, soybeans, vegetables, and meat or chicken meal. Extra fat, vitamins, and minerals are added to create a complete and balanced diet. Dry food is especially good for the teeth, because chewing helps scrape off plaque and tartar. However, you may want to soften it by adding warm water to feed a young puppy.

Problems with dry foods occur mainly in less expensive

Water is an equally crucial factor as food in your puppy's daily diet.

brands. These may be difficult to digest, leading to nutritional deficiencies. Some brands are also too low in fat for growing dogs. Always check the expiration date on the package and make certain the bag is in good condition. If fat has soaked through, the food may be contaminated or rancid.

Another popular product is canned meat or ration dinners. Meat foods contain mostly meat and meat by-products, along with soy nuggets known as textured vegetable protein. These chunks, colored brown or red, are easy to mistake for meat if you're unfamiliar with canned food.

Because meat dinners contain more protein and fat than other foods, they are beneficial when your puppy's energy needs are high. Although meat products should not be fed exclusively because they may not contain all of the nutrients needed for growth, a small amount can be added to dry food to improve its taste. Ration dinners, on the other hand, offer a balanced blend of ingredients, including vitamins and minerals. Depending on the variety you choose, ration products are suitable for all stages of life. Always store open cans in the refrigerator and don't leave uneaten food in your puppy's bowl.

The third formula, soft-moist dinner, is a relatively new addition to the array of available pet foods. Shaped like hamburger patties or meat chunks, soft-moist products combine fresh meat with grains or soybeans, vitamins and minerals, fat, and water to form a flavorful, easy-to-digest diet. These foods are convenient, easy to store, and carry well during travel. They are ideal for smaller breeds that need only one package per feeding. Because they don't require refrigeration, manufacturers usually add preservatives and humectants to prevent spoiling and drying. Sensitive puppies may not tolerate these additives (including sugar) and develop diarrhea or vomiting.

Some owners believe that home cooking offers the best diet for their puppies. However, with the variety of commercial foods available on the market, and companies' ongoing commitment to nutritional research, there is little reason to prepare food from scratch. Not only is it expensive and time consuming, but you also run the risk of leaving out ingredients, overfeeding, or creating foods with serious nutritional imbalances.

It's important to decide in the beginning what diet you prefer and stay with it. If you want to switch from the breeder's recommended food to a different type, make the change gradually. Mix a little of the new food with the old food, adding more of the new food until your puppy is eating it exclusively. You can reduce any problems associated with changing to an adult diet, when the time comes, by choosing a food in the same product line as the puppy food.

The chef has prepared a real smorgasbord for this party of Shibas!

This growing Chesapeake Bay Retriever puppy offers a subtle hint that it just may be dinner time!

CHOOSING A DOG BOWL

Did you know there are different types of bowls for different breeds? If your puppy has a short nose, like a Boston Terrier or Pug, you'll need to purchase a flat, shallow dish. Long-nosed breeds can use a deep bowl. Dogs with long ears, like Cocker Spaniels, do best with a narrow, steep-sided dish to keep their ears from falling in the food and water. Bowls come in different materials, too. You'll find them in metal, plastic, and ceramic. Before you bring your puppy home, be sure you have water and food bowls. Metal or plastic dishes work best, because they can't be chewed or broken. The size you need will depend on how big your pet will grow and how much food he will eat as an adult.

FEEDING SUGGESTIONS

- Choose a quiet, out-of-the-way place to feed your puppy and always feed him in the same place.
- Don't disturb your puppy when he's eating.
- Don't serve food directly from the refrigerator or stove. Be careful of foods prepared in the microwave oven. These may be too hot for your pet.
- Give your puppy about 20 minutes to eat, then remove any leftover dinner.
- If your puppy leaves food, feed a little less the next time. If he eats all his food and still looks hungry, add a little more at the next meal.
- Always provide fresh drinking water, but don't give your puppy cold water.
- Clean all bowls daily with hot water and soap and rinse thoroughly.

FEEDING FOR GROWTH

Puppies need twice the level of nutrients, per pound of body weight, as adults. However, their stomachs are too small to handle this much food at one time. If you have a toy breed puppy, you'll need to feed him three times a day until six months of age, then twice a day. You may consider a food specially designed for little dogs. These have smaller nuggets and are easier to chew than traditional foods.

Medium-size and large dogs should be fed twice a day until they are a year old. Giant-breed puppies often don't reach maturity until two years, so you may need to offer two meals a day until about 18 months. Foods are also available to meet the special requirements of large breeds.

Your puppy's breeder is one of the best sources for help in determining how much to feed. He or she has raised the puppies for at least eight weeks and has carefully studied their growth patterns. The veterinarian can also provide information on diets. Keep in mind that each puppy is an individual. Depending on his activity level and temperament, he may consume more or less than similar puppies—even his own littermates.

Use the directions on the food package only as a guideline. You may have to vary the amount you feed. Your puppy's condition is the best test in deciding how much food he needs. Ideally, you should be able to feel a layer of flesh (not fat) covering the puppy's ribs. You can note any changes by regularly weighing your pet and adjusting your feeding program accordingly.

It's important to remember that as a puppy grows, so does his need for a larger collar.

Teach your puppy good eating habits now and you'll be rewarded with a healthy adult dog later.

The most serious concern is overfeeding. Instead of helping your puppy grow into a mature dog, excessive feeding actually causes many problems in development. Because it produces abnormal growth, overfeeding may lead to knee and elbow disorders, splay feet, and lameness. Hip dysplasia in large breeds occurs at an earlier age, more often—and more severely— amongst puppies who consume too many calories. Mineral imbalances also predispose animals to hip dysplasia.

Another result of overfeeding is obesity. More dogs than ever before are overweight, which leads to heart and kidney problems, cancer, reproductive disorders, and lower resistance to disease. Because fat cells are growing in both size and number during puppyhood, overfeeding can cause a lifelong battle with obesity.

If you must add table scraps to your pet's food, use only a tiny amount of lean beef or chicken, potato or rice, or cooked vegetables. Add these directly to the bowl. Never feed from the table because this encourages begging. However, cut back on treats and biscuits if your puppy gains too much weight.

Correct feeding provides the foundation on which your puppy will grow to his full potential as a beloved companion, show dog, working dog, or canine athlete. The type of food you feed your pet, and the quality of nutrients play a critical role in the puppy's development. In fact, many kennel owners believe that proper feeding is the most significant aspect in raising dogs. By selecting a food that meets these complex nutritional requirements—and feeding the proper amount— you will be taking an important step in helping your puppy become a healthy adult.

Be sure to supply your puppy's outdoor home with plenty of fresh water.

LOOKING GOOD IS FEELING GOOD

Grooming is a natural activity for dogs. Wild dogs, such as foxes and wolves, groom each other to reinforce their positions within the pack. Domestic dogs also participate in grooming behavior. If you have more than one dog, you'll often see one licking and cleaning the other. When your puppy was a newborn, his mother handled all necessary grooming. By taking over these duties, you can strengthen the bond you have with your new pet.

Complete grooming includes brushing, bathing, toenail clipping, skin care, tooth cleaning, and ear care. Some breeds also require trimming, clipping, or stripping to keep their coats in proper condition. Grooming not only improves your puppy's appearance, but also plays a major role in good health. The regular attention you give your pet will allow you to notice changes and obtain prompt veterinary care when needed.

Begin simple grooming as soon as your puppy joins the household. The earlier you begin, the easier it will be to train your pet to accept handling. A grooming table is an ideal surface for dogs of all sizes. However, you can also use a sturdy table or counter with a nonslip mat. Place your puppy on the table and give him a few moments to sniff and look around. Then, carefully go over the coat with a soft brush or grooming glove. Keep these early sessions short and enjoyable.

Look in your puppy's ears, check his eyes, and gently touch his feet and toenails. However, don't clip the nails now. Develop a routine that you use each time you groom. For example, start with the feet and legs and finish with

A look into your dog's eyes can reveal the sweetness of his soul as well as the status of his overall health.

the head and ears. Hold one hand on your puppy when he's on the table and *never* leave him alone. You may need to work with an assistant if your pet is rambunctious. Always end the grooming session with a treat or play period. Remember, your little dog wants to please you. With gentleness, patience, and persistence, you'll soon have a pet who accepts and even enjoys grooming.

BRUSHING

An essential part of grooming is consistent brushing. Brushing distributes natural oils throughout the coat and prevents tangles and mats. It helps keep the skin healthy by stimulating blood circulation. Brushing also reduces the problems that accompany seasonal shedding by removing dead hair from the coat. To keep your puppy in peak condition, you'll need to brush his coat at least several times a week. Animals who have long or soft coats may require daily grooming.

Be sure to choose the right brush. Dogs with short hair, for example, need a stiff-bristled brush, hound glove, or grooming mitt. Long-haired breeds do best with a pin brush or curved wire slicker. Dogs with double coats, and terriers, require regular slicker brushes. These come in different sizes for small, medium, and large animals. Curly-coated breeds, like Poodles, take a slicker, bristle, or pin brush. If you're unsure of the proper brush to use, check with the breeder.

Your puppy should stand when you brush his legs. However, he may lie down while you do his back, ears, and head. Take a small section of hair at a time and brush all the way to the skin. With a short-haired or double-coated dog, first brush back to front against the growth pattern. This will loosen dead hair and dandruff. Then, brush with the growth to smooth the coat. To get through long hair, gently part the coat with your fingers and brush outward from the skin. Be careful not to brush the skin, itself, especially with a wire brush. This could hurt your puppy and irritate his sensitive skin. After you have thoroughly gone over the coat, use a blunt-toothed comb to check for tangles.

If you find that a tangle or mat has formed, take care of it right away. These are very uncomfortable and may lead to skin problems. To remove a mat, which is actually a tight, twisted mass of dead hair, work very slowly with the end tooth of a comb. Separate a few hairs at a time until you get through the mat.

Another method is to trim the tangle with sharp scissors or a mat comb. Start at the base of the mat and cut outward, away from the skin, toward the tip of the hair. Make two or three cuts paral-lel to the hair shafts. This will usually release the loose hair so you can comb it. You can also try one of the detangling lotions on the market. Satu-rate the mat for several minutes, then gently comb it out. Work only a few minutes at a time and always consider your puppy's comfort during grooming.

BATHING

Once you have thoroughly brushed the coat, your pet is ready for a bath. How often you bathe your puppy de-pends on coat type and whether your dog tends to get dirty. For example, white puppies usually need more frequent baths than dark-haired dogs. Certain breeds with hard or harsh coats, like terriers, can go several months between baths if they receive regular brushing. Dogs with soft, silky hair may need washing every few weeks. Bathing also helps to remove the shedding under-coat of double-coated breeds. If your puppy requires profes-sional grooming, he'll usually receive a bath at the same time.

Before you begin, assemble all the supplies you'll need so you won't have to run after them with a wet puppy in tow. These include shampoo, faucet attachment, washcloth, towels, nonslip mat, and hair dryer. First, wet the hair from back to front with warm water. Save the head and ears for last. Speak softly and reassuringly to make the experience as pleasant as possible. Apply a dab of shampoo to the coat and lather the rear legs, feet, and tail. Be sure to soap right down to the skin. The best kind of shampoo for young dogs is a mild, tearless, protein shampoo. Human shampoos are not suitable for pets.

Next, move to the back, chest, and front legs. Care-fully wet the head, keeping the water out of the ears, eyes, and nostrils. Some owners place cotton balls in their puppies' ears to protect the canals from soapy water. Finally, clean the face with a wet washcloth.

The most important part of the bath is the rinse. Make sure the water runs clear, without a trace of soap, and the hair feels squeaky clean. If you have a long-haired breed, you might want to apply conditioner to the coat. Let it stay on for two or three minutes, then rinse well. Wrap a large towel around your puppy and pat him dry. This may be enough to dry a short-haired breed. However, most dogs need the help of a hair dryer. Set the dryer on

Your puppy will be much more inclined to enjoy a bath if you remember to hold him gently, and speak reassuringly throughout the bathing process.

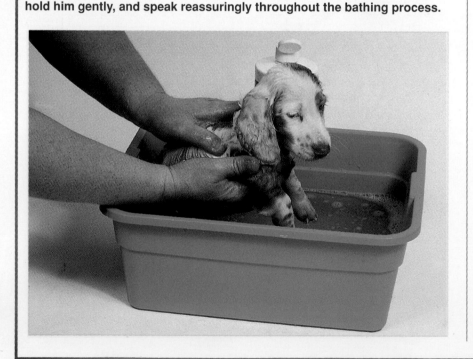

Despite the look on this big puppy's face, dogs actually *do* feel better after a bath!

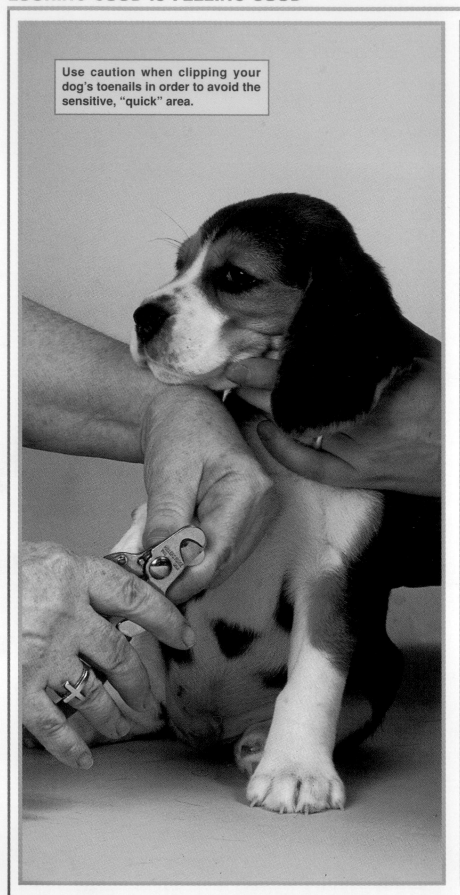

Use caution when clipping your dog's toenails in order to avoid the sensitive, "quick" area.

low or medium heat—never hot—and begin with the rear legs and back. Hold the dryer with one hand as you brush with the other. Move the dryer over the coat until the hair is completely dry and fluffy. Keep your puppy warm after his bath to avoid a chill.

TOENAIL CLIPPING

Although most dogs hate to have their toenails trimmed, this is a vital part of grooming that should not be overlooked. If you hear clicking when your puppy walks on the floor, the nails are too long and may break during play or exercise. Neglected animals sometimes have nails that curve into their feet, crippling them. Your pet's nails are different from yours, however. Dogs have a *quick*, or sensitive area containing nerves and a blood supply that runs the length of their nails. Breeds with white nails have a visible pink line that extends almost to the tip of the nail. The quick is more difficult to see in dogs with black nails.

Because the nail will hurt and bleed if you cut the quick, clip only the part of the nail that curves downward. Never trim more than one-eighth of an inch. If you accidentally nick the quick, apply a pinch of styptic powder, such as Kwik-Stop, to the tip of the nail. Hold the powder on the nail for a few seconds until the bleeding stops. After you have clipped all the nails, including dewclaws if present, smooth the rough edges with a nail file or emery board. Do only one foot at a time if your puppy is upset. To keep the nails at the proper length, clip them every two to three weeks.

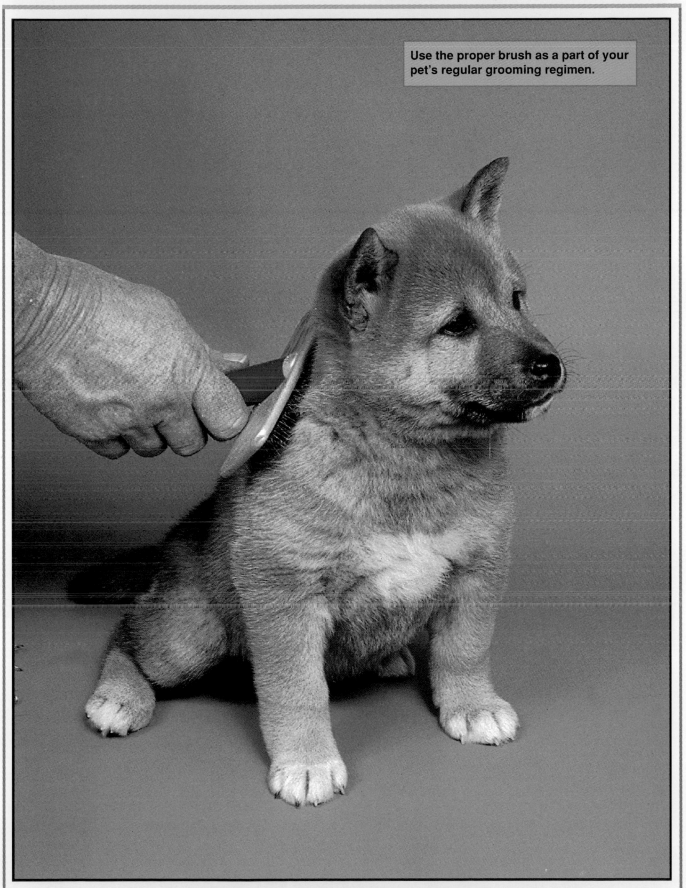

Use the proper brush as a part of your pet's regular grooming regimen.

FLEAS & TICKS

During your regular brushing sessions, take a close look at your puppy's skin. It should be clean and healthy, with no flaking, redness, or sores. If you notice your pet scratching more than usual, especially near the tail or rear legs, he may have a problem with fleas. However, you probably won't find them on your puppy.

Because fleas have a remarkable ability to jump, they spend most of their time off the dog, nestled in carpets, bedding, and grass. Their classic calling card is the black specks of feces they leave behind in the fur. The most common flea to affect pets is *Ctenocephalides felis*, or cat flea. Fleas not only produce intense itching and discomfort, but can also transmit tapeworms and several infectious diseases. Although infestations usually occur in warm, humid climates, fleas are found even in the dry areas of the Southwest.

Preventing and controlling fleas may seem like a never-ending challenge. To effectively win the battle on fleas, you must treat the animal, as well as the house and yard. Products for treating puppies include shampoos, dips, powders, foams, and collars. Some of the newer insecticides are applied directly to the skin, usually in a spot between the puppy's shoulder blades. These reportedly kill adult fleas within 24 hours and continue to work for up to three months. Perhaps the most promising advance is PROGRAM™, a prescription-only, once-a-month, flea-control tablet given orally to dogs. According to the manufacturer, PROGRAM™ works when a female flea bites a treated dog and passes the active ingredient to her eggs. By curbing a key step in the reproductive process, flea eggs can't develop and the life cycle is broken. To rid your house and yard of fleas, try using a fogger or spray. Take your puppy away from home before you spray. Wash all bedding materials and vacuum the carpet thoroughly.

Ticks are other pests that feed on dogs. The most common ticks are the brown dog tick, American dog tick, and deer tick. Ticks can carry Rocky Mountain Spotted Fever, typhus, and Lyme disease. Tick bites may also cause skin sores and occasionally even tick paralysis. Puppies pick up ticks in tall grass, shrubbery, or wooded areas. However, animals like birds, mice, and deer often bring them right into your backyard.

Always check your puppy carefully after a walk in woods or fields. If you find a tick embedded in the skin, grasp it with tweezers or your fingers, as close to the skin as possible, and pull straight up with steady pressure. Clean the area well with alcohol. To help release the tick, saturate a cotton ball with alcohol and hold it on the tick before you try to remove it. Talk to your veterinarian about the proper time for a Lyme disease vaccination. Depending on where you live, fleas and ticks may be an occasional annoyance or a chronic problem. Fortunately, a variety of treatments are available to help you win the war.

Being outdoors will expose your puppy to insects and other potentially harmful critters.

DENTAL CARE

Puppies acquire their baby teeth, consisting of the incisors (front teeth), canines (fangs), and premolars, by six weeks of age. Between 12 and 14 weeks, they start to go through the uncomfortable teething stage. During this process, which lasts several months, the first set loosens and falls out as the permanent teeth emerge.

Watch your puppy's mouth during this stage. Sometimes a temporary tooth doesn't come out when a permanent tooth appears. In this case, the veterinarian should remove the baby tooth so the bite will develop correctly. Some puppies experience a lot of discomfort when teething. Others go through the process with few noticeable signs. If your youngster seems to be in pain, offer a biscuit, toy, or frozen washcloth for him to chew on for relief.

Until recently, many owners were unaware that they needed to clean their dogs' teeth. Although veterinarians have known that the buildup of tartar can lead to gum disease and tooth loss, they also realize that the bacteria that form in the dog's mouth can spread to other parts of his body, contributing to heart and kidney disease and other serious illnesses. To keep your puppy's teeth in good shape, begin a program of regular brushing as soon as the permanent set comes in. One method of cleaning involves wrapping a piece of gauze around your index finger, dipping it in doggie toothpaste, and rubbing it carefully over the teeth. You also can use a toothbrush designed for dogs. For small

Supplying the puppy with safe, durable Nylabone® products will help him through his teething stage.

puppies, try a cat toothbrush that has bristles only at the tip. There also are several oral rinses on the market that fight bacteria as they freshen breath.

You can train your puppy to accept handling of his mouth by proceeding gently and slowly. Praise lavishly when your pet behaves. However, despite regular care at home, some animals—especially those who eat soft food—have such a problem with tartar that it must be removed by a veterinarian with special tools and toothpastes. Because dogs usually won't hold still to have their teeth cleaned, the procedure is performed under a safe, short-acting anesthesia. Be sure to follow up with a consistent program of brushing at home.

EAR CARE

Another area that requires attention is the ears. Are they clean and odor-free? Is there any wax or discharge? If you notice your puppy scratching his ears or shaking his head, he may have an infection or allergy. Infections often come from water in the ears during bath time, excess wax, or throat or respiratory infections that travel to the ears. Allergies come from substances in the environment, like grasses, shampoo, pollen, or dust mites. Others may be associated with the food your puppy eats. All conditions require veterinary attention. If you don't treat an infection, it can spread to the middle or inner ear and this may cause pain, a ruptured eardrum, or even nerve damage or deafness.

Breeds with long, hanging ears are more likely to develop ear infections than those with upright ears. This is because air can't freely circulate, making an ideal environment for bacteria to grow. Keep the ears clean by wiping the inside of the flap and ear canal opening with a cotton ball soaked in cleaning solution. Don't probe inside the canal, especially with swabs, because this can push waxy material deeper. Poodles, and certain other breeds, have hair that grows in the ear canal, which further hinders air circulation. This should be removed every few weeks by carefully plucking a few strands at a time with tweezers. Pull only the hair that grows inside the canal, not on the inside of the flap. If you take your dog to a professional groomer, he or she should clean out this hair.

Another common ear problem is mites. The microscopic mites that affect the ears cause intense itching, scratching, and head shaking. Another mite that attacks puppies is the scabies mite. These, too, produce itching and raw, crusty patches around the tips of the ears. Because mites can travel to other parts of the body and other pets in the household, your puppy should be treated by the veterinarian with appropriate medication.

Grooming provides a marvelous time for you to bond with your pet.

PROFESSIONAL GROOMING

Many dogs require specialized grooming to produce the distinctive appearance of the breed. Terriers are often hand plucked or stripped to remove dead hair and preserve the color and texture of their coats. Poodles, with their curly, nonshedding coats, need regular clipping or scissoring to maintain their elegant demeanors. Long-haired breeds require regular trimming to tidy their overall look. Although it's possible to master these skills at home, many owners prefer to take their dogs to professional groomers.

To find a qualified groomer, start by asking the breeder or veterinarian for recommendations. Many animal clinics include grooming as part of their services. This offers the advantage of medical care in case of an emergency and the convenience of one-stop shopping for medicines or pet foods. Also, check with friends or neighbors who take their dogs for professional grooming.

Once you have the names of two or three shops, call ahead to schedule a preliminary interview. Don't take your puppy with you on this visit. When you meet the groomer, find out what experience he or she has with your particular breed. The best Poodle groomer in the world won't help if you need your terrier hand plucked for the show ring. Has he attended grooming school? Does she have any special certification? Notice whether the shop is clean, odor-free, and well lighted. Is the groomer careful and gentle with the dogs? Does the shop have adequate

The effort you put into bathing and grooming your pet will be reflected in his stance and demeanor.

kennel facilities for holding pets?

Communicate clearly about the type of haircut you want. Some dog clubs have prepared comprehensive booklets or videos on the proper way to groom their breeds. Also, find out about the costs involved in grooming. Depending on the breed, the dog's size, and how much needs to be done, this could range from $25 to $50. Complete grooming should include bathing and drying, trimming or clipping, cutting the nails, and cleaning the ears. However, for your puppy's first visit, schedule only a bath and light trim. Avoid "the works" until he has

become adjusted to the various procedures involved and gains confidence in the groomer.

Whether you enlist the help of a salon or care for your pet at home, regular grooming is an important part of responsible ownership. Puppies who are well-groomed not only look good, but also feel good. Their whole attitude changes. Notice the bounce in your puppy's step as he takes his morning walk; the sparkle;\ in his eyes; the enthusiasm in his outlook. Grooming reinforces the special bond you share with your puppy, and is a significant factor in maintaining his health as well.

PUPPY HEALTH CARE

As a new owner, you'll probably find that you have many questions about the health of the little dog entrusted to your care. Each pet is different, with his own distinct habits and problems. The veterinarian is a vital ally in keeping your puppy well. If you don't already have a veterinarian, ians near your home. Some listings use the AAHA logo, which means the clinic meets the high standards of the American Animal Hospital Association.

Will you need boarding, grooming, or training services? Many hospitals offer a variety of services—even pet sitters and animal dieti- kept, clean, and relatively odor-free? Are the reception duties handled in a calm, efficient manner? Does the staff genuinely care about animals? Are the location and hours convenient?

Another factor to consider is the veterinarian's knowledge and experience with your breed, especially if it's

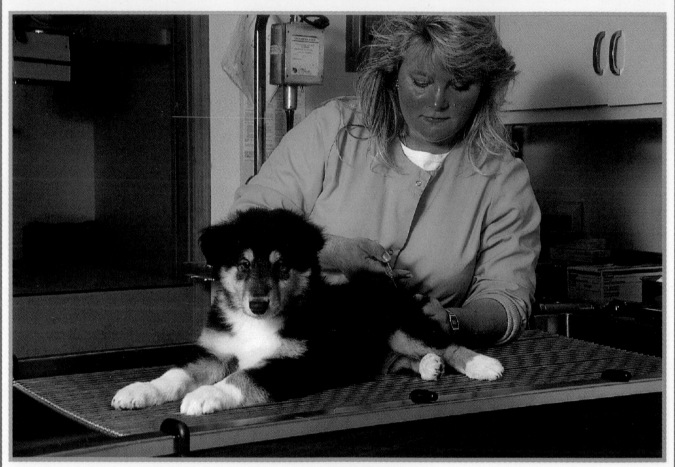

Regular visits to the veterinarian will ensure your pet's optimal health.

you'll want to choose one before you bring your pet home. The breeder may be able to recommend a clinic if you're buying locally. Other sources for referrals include professional groomers, humane organizations, veterinary associations, and dog-owning friends or neighbors. You also can check the yellow pages for veterinar- tians—for the convenience of their clients. Once you've narrowed your choices to two or three, call for an appointment to visit the facilities and talk with the doctors. During your visit, carefully observe the environment as well as the staff. Is this the kind of place you would want to bring your puppy? Is the building well- a rare breed or has special requirements. Some clinics have specialists on staff, although many doctors refer complex or difficult cases to the large teaching hospitals at veterinary colleges. Take your time and don't be afraid to ask questions. Your pet's well-being depends on the care he receives now and throughout his lifetime.

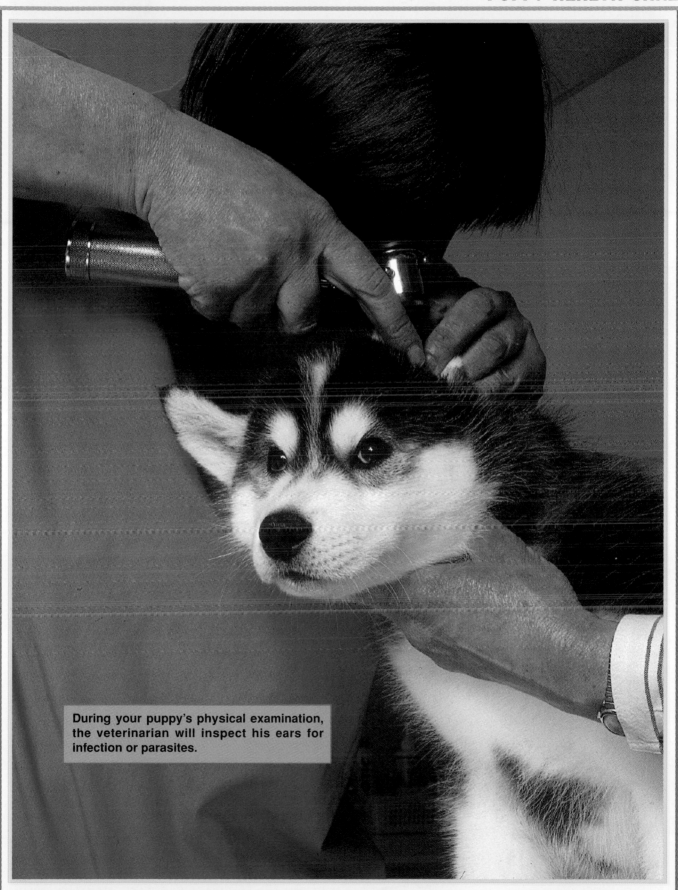

During your puppy's physical examination, the veterinarian will inspect his ears for infection or parasites.

Veterinarians often include the whole family in explaining proper care for your pet.

YOUR PUPPY'S FIRST EXAM

When you buy from a responsible breeder, you're selecting a dog with the belief that it's healthy and free of observable birth defects. Many breeders give written guarantees, offering a replacement or refund if a problem is found. Therefore, it's important to have your new pet examined as soon as possible—preferably within 48 to 72 hours.

During this initial visit, the veterinarian will carefully inspect your puppy for birth defects and problems that are known to occur in the breed. He or she will listen to the heart and lungs, feel for unusual lumps or bumps, examine the coat and skin, go over the legs and joints, and check the eyes, ears, and teeth. If you purchased a male puppy, the doctor will also examine the testicles to make sure both are fully descended in the scrotum. Although the testicles usually descend before birth, they can be retained in the abdomen as late as four to five months. This may require medical or surgical treatment. Be sure to take any records of previous vaccinations and wormings. Also, bring a fresh stool sample so the technician can determine whether additional worming is necessary.

This is your opportunity to ask questions about your puppy's health, as well as feeding, housebreaking, or training. Ask for the suggested schedule of vaccinations and discuss the doctor's recommendations on neutering your pet. Many veterinarians have brochures available on topics of interest. Some offer new-puppy kits, with food samples, booklets, and health charts. You'll find it very helpful to keep a record of doctor visits, noting your puppy's symptoms, medications, shots, or surgeries. A comprehensive medical reference, such as Dr. Lowell Ackerman's *Owner's Guide to Dog Health* (T.F.H. Publications, Inc.), is a must for all owners.

Most puppy care involves the prevention of illness, through vaccinations, parasite control, and proper diet. However, if the veterinarian does discover a problem,

Your veterinarian has the specific knowledge and trained eye to offer insight into your pet's health.

you'll have to decide whether to treat the condition or return the puppy to the breeder. This will depend on the severity of the illness and the prognosis for a good outcome. Puppies with difficulties like deafness can still make wonderful pets if their owners are willing to take extra time in training and handling. However, if your puppy has a major defect, you may save yourself months or years of heartbreak by taking the difficult step of returning him to the breeder.

The puppy that you hold in your hand today will quickly blossom into a handsome, healthy adult with the proper care. This is a Norfolk Terrier.

A puppy will never turn down the challenge of a new adventure!

VACCINATIONS

When a puppy is born, he receives temporary immunity to several infectious diseases from antibodies, or special protein molecules, in his mother's first milk. However, this protection lasts only a few weeks. By the time puppies are about six weeks old, they need to develop their own immune systems. Dogs, like people, form disease-fighting antibodies to certain illnesses after exposure to mild or altered forms of antigens, or foreign substances. The antibodies then circulate through the bloodstream, ready to mount a quick attack if specific bacteria or viral organisms invade the body. Although there is some degree of risk in any procedure, the safest way to expose animals to antigens is through a controlled series of vaccinations.

Your puppy probably will need to be inoculated every two to three weeks until about 16 to 20 weeks of age. Depending on the diseases that are present where you live, the vaccines usually include antigens for distemper, hepatitis, adenovirus, parvovirus, parainfluenza, and rabies. Keep in mind that until your pet is fully vaccinated, he's at high risk of contracting an infectious illness. Avoid taking a young dog to parks, training courses, dog show grounds, or other places where unfamiliar animals gather. Be cautious around wildlife, too. After your puppy reaches adulthood, it's important to schedule yearly booster shots to keep his immune system strong.

Puppies tend to wind up in the most extraordinary circumstances, so it's a good idea to have a trusted veterinarian in case of surprise accidents.

The goal of every breeder should be to provide each and every puppy with a safe and loving home.

NEUTERING YOUR PET

Another step you can take to help your dog stay well ranks second only to giving vaccinations in terms of importance: Neuter your puppy before he reaches sexual maturity. The operation, in which the sex organs are removed, is called spaying in females and castrating possibility of developing mammary, uterine, and ovarian cancers. It also prevents pyometra, a serious infection of the uterus that frequently occurs in older females. Spaying also avoids the twice-yearly heat cycles. The hormonal changes that dogs experience during these periods may be one of the disease, hormonal abnormalities, and perianal adenoma, which is a growth around the anus. Although neutering is considered major surgery, it's very safe—especially when animals are young and their reproductive organs are small and immature. Your puppy will recover quickly and usually will come home

Neutering your puppy allows for a more relaxed and even-tempered pet. These are a white Puli pup and adult.

in males. Not only does neutering avoid the possibility that a dog will become accidentally pregnant or sire an unwanted litter, but it also offers many additional benefits to a pet's physical and emotional well-being. For example, spaying a female by six months of age will nearly eliminate the risk factors in developing reproductive cancers.

Males, too, benefit from early castration. They are less likely to display unsuitable behavior, such as marking their territory, roaming, and showing aggression. Castration also helps to reduce the chances of testicular cancer, prostate the next day. He may be more tired than usual and want a quiet place to rest. Don't let your puppy run or jump for about a week. However, he soon will be playful and frisky again. (Neutered dogs can't compete in the conformation ring, but may participate in all obedience events.)

After exploring the Great Outdoors, carefully examine your puppy for ticks and other insects.

HOME VETERINARY KIT

gauze rolls	rectal thermometer
bandages	petroleum jelly
adhesive tape	Anti-diarrheal
scissors	Antacid
tweezers	Milk of Magnesia
cotton balls	dosing dropper
cotton swabs	activated charcoal tablets
3-percent hydrogen peroxide	

A First Aid kit will prepare you for almost any indoor or outdoor small emergency.

PUPPY AILMENTS

Anal Sac Problems

Puppies have a pair of anal sacs located on each side of the anus. Although their exact purpose is unknown, the secretion they produce may lubricate the rectum, allowing dogs to pass their bowel movements more easily. The distinctive scent may also help them determine the sex of other dogs. Sometimes the sacs don't empty fully and become impacted with material. When this happens, you might notice your puppy "scooting" across the floor or trying to lick the area. The veterinarian can express the fluid by gently pressing the sacs. If the sacs become infected, they can swell and rupture through the skin. These abscesses usually respond well to antibiotics, warm compresses, and mild pain medication.

Constipation

Puppies normally have a bowel movement after each meal—two or three a day. However, if your puppy routinely has fewer movements, it's no cause for concern. Dogs with constipation usually strain repeatedly or experience pain trying to have a movement. Constipation may occur if your puppy eats a low-fiber, canned-meat dinner, or when he overeats. It also results from eating indigestible material, such as grass, paper, or cloth.

Never give your puppy beef or chicken bones because they can fragment and cause fecal impaction. Even rawhides can lead to problems in some dogs. Always provide safe chew toys. Long-haired dogs sometimes have a problem when the hair forms a mat over the opening of the anus. Be sure to wash this area regularly and keep any long hair trimmed. For occasional bouts of constipation, give Milk of Magnesia or add a teaspoon of mineral oil to your puppy's dinner. Try changing to a food with a higher fiber content and make sure your puppy gets enough exercise. If constipation persists, contact the veterinarian.

Coughing

This can be caused by an allergy, sore throat, tonsillitis, worms, or lung or heart disease. Try to identify whether the cough is dry, moist, gagging, or wheezing. Although cough medicine relieves mild cases, veterinary treatment is needed when

Who's that peeking out from there?

Not every aspect of a puppy's welfare can be spelled out in black and white; he also requires lots of love and attention to give him that rosy glow.

This photo proves that you can—and should—lead a *dog* to water, but you can't force her to drink!

Because of his coat type, the Shar-Pei is susceptible to various skin problems.

coughing is accompanied by fever, nasal or eye discharge, vomiting, or difficulty breathing.

Dehydration

The loss of water and electrolytes (sodium, potassium, and chloride) often follows prolonged diarrhea, vomiting, fever, or heat exhaustion. Signs of dehydration include dryness of the mouth, sunken eyes, loss of skin elasticity, muscle twitching, and shock. Dehydration requires prompt medical attention. In its early stages, puppies respond to oral electrolyte replacement formulas like Pediatric STAT. If dehydration persists, they may need intravenous fluids.

Diarrhea

Diarrhea is fairly common in dogs, partly because their relatively short colons have difficulty absorbing all the fluids from undigested food in the intestines. Changes in your puppy's diet, infection, worms, allergies, and stress can cause diarrhea. For mild cases, withhold food for 12 to 24 hours, but provide ice cubes for water. Give one half to one teaspoon of anti-diarrheal or antacid medication every four to six hours. Follow with a bland diet of lean hamburger, cottage cheese, cooked egg, or rice. If you notice vomiting, fever, or blood in the feces—or if the diarrhea lasts longer than 36 hours—consult your veterinarian.

Hot Spots

Acute moist dermatitis, or hot spots, is a bacterial skin infection that frequently occurs in long-haired or double-coated breeds. An irritation—from fleas, allergies, or even a dirty coat—seems to trigger the problem. Too little fatty acid in the diet is also a factor. The problem is then compounded when the dog bites or scratches the area. Identified by their red, ulcerated lesions, hot spots spread rapidly to form large bare patches. Because the sores are so painful, the veterinarian may have to sedate the puppy to clip the hair from the wound. The area is then cleaned with surgical soap and an antibiotic or cortisone cream is applied. Sulfodene, available in pet supply stores, helps to heal hot spots when applied several times a day. Hot spots respond well to treatment and the hair usually grows back.

Insect Stings

Stings from bees, yellow jackets or ants may cause pain and swelling at the site of the sting. Clean the area with rubbing alcohol and remove the stinger, if there is one, with tweezers. Try not to squeeze the stinger or it will release more toxins. Make a paste of baking soda and water and apply it to the sting. Cold compresses or ice packs help reduce swelling. Some puppies are particularly sensitive to insect stings and may experience allergic reactions. Labored breathing, swelling of the tongue or loss of consciousness require immediate veterinary treatment.

Puppy Dermatitis

Puppies often develop the skin infections juvenile pyoderma, impetigo, and acne. Pyoderma, also called

puppy strangles, occurs most often in young dogs less than four months old. Signs include swelling of the lips, eyelids, face, and lymph nodes, along with crusty, infected sores around the face. Warm compresses help reduce the swellings. Cortisone medication or antibiotics also may be needed.

Impetigo, characterized by red patches and blisters, often starts on the hairless belly and groin areas. The blisters then rupture to form crusty, brown sores. The bacteria *staphylococci* are usually responsible for impetigo. However, puppies are more susceptible when they must fight the additional burden of poor diet, worms, or immune disorders. Impetigo responds well to medicated shampoos and antibiotics.

Another common condition is acne. These bumps or blackheads usually affect the chin and lower lip, and often occur in dogs with oily skins.

Treatment involves bathing the puppy with benzoyl peroxide shampoo and applying benzoyl peroxide cream to the affected areas. Oral antibiotics may also be needed. Usually, acne clears up by the time the puppy reaches his first birthday.

Vomiting

Puppies may vomit as a result of excitement, nervousness, motion sickness, worms, or overeating. Several serious illnesses, including distemper, hepatitis, pancreatitis, and ulcers, also cause vomiting. If your puppy vomits, but seems normal with no other signs of illness, the condition probably is not serious. Withhold food for 12 to 24 hours, but provide ice cubes for water. Feed a bland diet for a day or two and allow plenty of rest. If your puppy has a fever, diarrhea, vomits blood, or is sick for more than 24 hours, contact the veterinarian.

This mother Chinook looks as if she's keeping a careful eye on her youngsters. Grooming offers the opportunity to inspect your puppy for signs of illness, such as fleas, mites, and other cuts and bites.

This White German Shepherd pup's coat is healthy and lustrous thanks to a proper diet and regular grooming.

Your veterinarian is a trusted ally in ensuring your pet's health and well-being.

Worms

The most common worms affecting puppies are roundworms, hookworms, tapeworms, and whipworms. Puppies can acquire worms before birth, through nursing, or from contaminated soil or feces. Worms may also enter the body by eating raw meat or fish, or coming into contact with dead animals. Fleas play a role in the spread of tapeworms, serving as the intermediate host. Pets usually get worms by sniffing or licking infected material. However, the larval form of hookworms can penetrate the skin.

Because puppies may be born with worms, they should be wormed at two to three weeks of age and again at about five to six weeks. Be sure to bring a fresh stool sample to the first veterinary appointment. To prescribe the best treatment, if it's needed, the veterinarian must examine the specimen under a microscope to identify the kind of worm involved. He or she can then choose the safest product to use. Once your pet is free of worms, you can help prevent reinfestation by keeping your yard clean and free of feces. Also, avoid places where strange dogs gather. Worms are less of a problem in adults, because dogs seem to acquire some natural immunity that helps them fight off the parasites.

Another worm responsible for serious illness is the heartworm. Transmitted by a bite from a mosquito, rather than from dog-to-dog contact, heartworms are found throughout the United States and Canada. Adult heartworms live in the puppy's heart and large blood vessels, growing 4 to 12 inches long. This causes damage to the blood vessels, heart, and lungs. Because the worms can live for several years within the body, they breed thousands of tiny, microscopic worms, called microfilaria. When a mosquito bites a dog with these circulating microfilaria, it becomes infected and can transmit the worms through its stinger to another dog.

Dogs can have both adult and baby heartworms for many years without signs of the disease. By the time owners notice coughing, lack of energy, difficulty breathing, and weight loss, their pets are very ill. Treatment, aimed at killing both adult worms and microfilaria, has many potential complications.

Fortunately, heartworms can be prevented by using one of the prescription medicines now on the market. However, these preventives can cause dangerous reactions if heartworms are already present. Currently, two types of tests can detect heartworms. The first, in which a blood sample is examined under a microscope, shows microfilaria circulating in the blood. This suggests the presence of adult worms, but does not discern them directly. A newer test, called an antigen test, detects a specific antigen produced by adult female heartworms. Dogs that have never taken preventive medication should receive both tests before the first dose. The antigen test should be done yearly, before starting the next season's medication. The best age to begin heartworm prevention, especially if you live in a region with a heavy infestation of mosquitoes, is between 9 and 12 weeks of age. Your pet can safely take Heartgard 30™, a once-a-month pill or chewable tablet, or Filaribits™, a daily chewable. (Collies and collie mixes should not take Heartgard 30™ products.) These may be taken year round or at least one to two months before and after mosquito season. Newer heartworm medicines also help to combat hookworms, roundworms, and whipworms.

IN SUMMARY

Raising a healthy puppy requires the active involvement of three individuals: the breeder, the veterinarian, and the owner. The breeder played an important role in the birth of your healthy puppy. He or she carefully screened the bloodline for hereditary diseases, made sure the parent dogs were fit and sound, and provided ideal conditions for your puppy to develop into the handsome youngster who stole your heart. The veterinarian provides the specialized knowledge, skill, and care your puppy needs to stay well.

You have done your part, too. You've created a home environment where your puppy is safe and secure. You offer nourishing food so your best friend can grow strong and mighty. You groom your puppy regularly to help him look and feel good. As you have discovered from reading this *yearBOOK*, there are many responsibilities involved in owning a pet. However, the time and effort you invest in caring for your puppy will be more than repaid in the abundance of unconditional love your dog gives you in return.

SUGGESTED READING

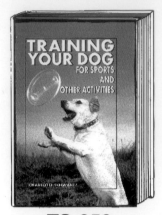

TS-258
TRAINING YOUR DOG FOR SPORTS AND OTHER ACTIVITIES

TS-214
OWNER'S GUIDE TO DOG HEALTH

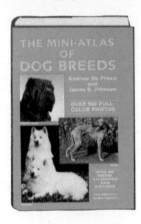

H-1106
MINI-ATLAS OF DOG BREEDS

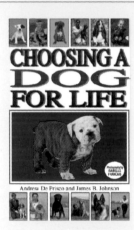

TS-257
CHOOSING A DOG FOR LIFE

TS-283
TRAINING PROBLEM DOGS

JG-109
TRAINING THE PERFECT PUPPY

Acknowledgement

This volume in the Basic Training, Caring & Understanding Library series was researched in part at the Ontario Veterinary college at the University of Guelph in Guelph, Ontario, and was published under the auspices of Dr. Herbert R. Axelrod.

A world-renown scientist, explorer, author, university professor, lecturer, and publisher, Dr. Axelrod is the best-known tropical fish expert in the world and the founder and chairman of T.F.H. Publications, Inc., the largest and most respected publisher of pet literature in the world. He has written 16 definitive texts on Ichthyology (including the best-selling Handbook of Tropical Aquarium Fishes), published more than 30 books on individual species of fish for the hobbyist, written hundreds of articles, and discovered hundreds of previously unknown species, six of which have been named after him.

Dr. Axelrod holds a Ph.D and was awarded an Honorary Doctor of Science degree by the University of Guelph, where he is now an adjunct professor in the Department of Zoology. He has served on the American Pet Products Manufacturers Association Board of Governors and is a member of the American Society of Herpetologists and Ichthyologists, the Biometric Society, the New York Zoological Society, the New York Academy of Sciences, the American Fisheries Society, the National Research Council, the National Academy of Sciences, and numerous aquarium societies around the world. In 1977, Dr. Axelrod was awarded the Smithson Silver Medal for his ichthyological and charitable endeavors by the Smithsonian Institution. A decade later, he was elected an endowment member of the American Museum of Natural History and was named a life member of the James Smithson Society by the Smithsonian Associates' national board. He has donated in excess of $50 million in recent years to the American Museum of National History, the University of Guelph, and other institutions.

Index